# PALINDROME

*Pauletta Hansel*

"The present rips apart and joins together again;
it begins; it is beginning itself.
It has a past, but in the form of remembrance.
It has a history, but it is not history."

—Emmanuel Levinas,
*Time and the Other*

DOS MADRES

2017

# DOS MADRES PRESS INC.

P.O. Box 294, Loveland, Ohio 45140
www.dosmadres.com    editor@dosmadres.com

Dos Madres is dedicated to the belief that the small press is essential to the vitality of contemporary literature as a carrier of the new voice as well as the older, sometimes forgotten voices of the past. And in an ever more virtual world, to the creation of fine books pleasing to the eye and hand.

Dos Madres is named in honor of Vera Murphy and Libbie Hughes, the "Dos Madres" whose contributions have made this press possible.

Dos Madres Press, Inc., is an Ohio Not For Profit Corporation and a 501(c)(3) qualified public charity. Contributions are tax deductible.

Executive Editor: Robert J. Murphy

Illustration & Book Design: Elizabeth H. Murphy
www.illusionstudios.net

Typeset in Adobe Garamond Pro & Dali
ISBN 978-1-939929-82-2
Library of Congress Control Number: 2017944662

This project was supported in part by the Ohio Arts Council, which receives support from the State of Ohio and the National Endowment for the Arts.

**Ohio Arts**
COUNCIL

### First Edition

Published by Dos Madres Press, Inc.

# INTRODUCTION

*Palindrome* is a book of poems written in response to
my mother's dementia. To say it is the most personal of my col-
lections is perhaps an overstatement, given that my poems are
usually drawn from the wells of experience and memory. I will
say that it is my only book written mostly in present tense. Not
Wordsworth's "emotion recollected in tranquility" but crafted
within my ongoing experience of a mother in the midst of a
devastating change.

"Crafted" is a word I use with intention. Once these
poems amassed a collective heft, I knew I was looking at my
next manuscript. I was mindful that the personal subject mat-
ter—dementia and caregiving—might well overwhelm the
literary nature of the project. And yet it was the attention to
the craft of poetry that allowed this work to come into being,
that allowed me the creative distance to make meaning even as
I engaged daily with a disease process that took my mother's
meaning-making ability away. I am not a formal poet by incli-
nation or training, and yet "a formal feeling came" as I worked
with the material this ongoing loss was giving me, and sonnets,
syllabic forms and palindromes are woven throughout.

As a poet and as a daughter, I wanted my mother to be
in this book—not just the mother in the "now" of the poems,
but a more integrated representation of all she has been and
has become. I had written many poems about her life and ours
together, but those are in other books and don't belong here.
As it turned out, my mother had already solved this problem
for me. When cleaning out her house after the move to the
dementia unit, my sister found 500+ pages of Mom's handwrit-
ten letters to our father from the year after his death. Her grief
journal, yes, but also her memoirs which, she wrote in one of
her last letters, she hoped her children would someday find and
read. Knowing me as she did, she must have known if I found
them I would use them. This book includes blank verse sonnet

sequences drawn directly from my mother's writing; I am grateful for her voice within these pages.

And, of course, I trust (as I must when I send work out to find its readers) that there is more to find in this collection of poems than my mother's life and mine, but something too of the nature of memory, time and human connection—with all their switchbacks and reversals, forming a sort of palindrome.

Pauletta Hansel
2017

# TABLE OF CONTENTS

## She Made Everything

## The Long Way Home

# Who Do I Think I Am?

# The Real Story

## She Made Everything

## My Mother Has Stopped Telling Me
### She Loves Me

Look at us now.
My mother finally bound
to her wheelchair (that's how
they like it in the nursing home).
She thinks she is walking,
one foot and then the other,
her lumbering four-wheeled
body follows, and behind her
trails Miss Push-Me-Pull-Me—
that's what she muttered at me yesterday,
a sudden spark that flew my meddling hands
down from the handles of her chair.
And even when we sit together,
fingers entwined, she pushes back away,
I pull her toward me,
memorize her face,
the folds beside her eyes,
the lips that purse now
for a kiss, a dab of oatmeal
in one corner. I say,
I love you, Mom,
and then she's off again;
we dangle one side and the other
of the teeter-totter air.

## She Made Everything

we had: winter coats and Barbie doll purses, yeast rolls,
cornbread, a teddybear cake for my third birthday, dresses
with rickrack on the collars and the hems that matched
her own, my brother's Batman cape. A gown for a minia-
ture Kentucky first lady that sits somewhere in a museum.
Candles, doughnuts, soupbeans for my father, jello salad
with mayonnaise in the middle and maraschino cher-
ries. My aunt's wedding cake. A Bavarian torte without a
recipe. Punch in a crystal bowl. She upholstered our furni-
ture, rewired our lamps, "antiqued" the wooden tables
she bought from the thrift store (later she would wish she
hadn't). She built my father's first bookcases from polished
boards and bricks and thin rods of metal that she threaded
through the holes of the bricks and the holes in the boards
she had drilled to line up exactly. Those rods held the con-
traption together, and even then I knew she was the one
held us together like a strong spine.

## Portrait of My Mother's Dementia as Saturn's Rings

The shattered skins
of ancient moons
that bind her.

# Palindrome

If time, too, is a place
 we journey slowly through as
  for a closer look, might not
   (we ask) these tracks we travel
    take us back again,
     the way my mother remembers,
      now, the future, lives in the past?

      Now the future lives in the past
     the way my mother remembers.
    Take us back again.
   We ask these tracks we travel
  for a closer look. Might not
 we journey slowly through as
if time, too, is a place?

## Union Terminal: The Whispering Fountain

Inside the rotunda, I can only
think of the past. My mother as a girl
of twelve stood twice where I stand,
passing through in 1944
from the creekbeds of Kentucky
on her way to Buffalo—Niagara River
and the great lake's shores—
and back again in '45. Now
my husband and I wheel her all around it.
She told me once what she liked best
to see on the trip North were all
the pretty dresses, cut on a bias
with hems up almost to the knees,
saving fabric for the war effort.
Now whatever she remembers
about this or anywhere she's been
is locked inside her brain.
I send her with my husband
to the fountain one side of the rotunda,
and from the other call, "Hello!"
My voice is carried up along
the grooves of the dome and back
down to her. I am calling
to the past. She doesn't answer.

## Aphasia

My mother forgets the words
she means to say
and I forget to listen
to what she cannot tell me.

# My Mother Remembers Buffalo, 1944-45

That year, sixth grade, Miss Shaw from the mission
down on Cutshin got me a place at a church
lady's house near the lake at the top
of the map she kept rolled above her desk.
Buffalo is where I learned to snap my words
closed tight before the jeers got in between
the syllables one Kentucky vowel
could make. I slept in a room with the other
girls the mission folks swept North to school
the mountains from us. I don't know where all
they came from. We weren't to speak of home unless
to say how much better city life was.
And it was easier. We walked to school
on sidewalks in clothes that kept the cold out.

Back home we'd tuck our dresses up to walk
through mud and, if the creek was high, we'd jump
stone to stone to keep our feet from soaking.
In Buffalo at night I'd see soldiers
by the streetlamps kissing their pretty girls,
lines painted on their calves like they were stockings
those big stores would sell before the war.
Every day another star was on
another door, another son or father dead.
Forty stars while I was there. I wonder
still how it could be, those houses side by
side so close a body could call down from
their window how they're sorry for the death,
except they never knew each other's names.

The day I learned my little brother
Jimmy died was February 20,
1945. The war was coming
to an end and too my year in Buffalo.
No doctor to say why at six he was
no more than three feet tall, stomach wide
as his height. I cried until I couldn't cry,
and then I slept. Next day I wrote a letter,
at the bottom put what I was not to:
"I want to come home. You mustn't say so."
Well, of course, Dad couldn't keep his mouth closed;
he told Miss Shaw, she told the church lady who
pulled me by my hair down to the basement,
beat me with a yardstick till my legs bled.

Jimmy's illness never did affect his mind.
He could read and write from books I'd bring home
to teach him. Mom was afraid she'd have to
send him to school, sick as he was, once he
turned seven. After I left, he got too weak
to worry about that. Dad took no help;
they'd not use his boy as a guinea pig.
In the end, Jimmy went to Frontier Nurses
and from Hyden took the long train ride to
Cincinnati Children's all alone. From there
what happened is unknown to me. When Dad
raised money up to go he went straight
to a room with Jimmy dead that morning. He's
buried by the chapel up from Cutshin Creek.

On Valentine's, before I knew, I'd sent
Jimmy all the cards my school friends gave me.
There they were when finally I got home, but
he was not. I told Miss Shaw myself I'd
not go back to Myrtle, that was her name.
She'd made us write with scratch and carry our
ink in a bottle. We were twelve, alone,
kindness was what we needed. Still, not all
in Buffalo had her meanness. Everywhere
there's people carting more than they can hold.
The day FDR died, my friend's brother
threw himself over Glen Falls, draft notice by
his bed. He'd helped me ice skate. I could feel
his hands holding me up long after he died.

While I was gone the war had come to Cutshin
and to Pilgrims Knob, Virginia, where Mom's
people stayed. I lost two first cousins in
Kentucky, two across the mountain; three
of Mother's brothers still were in the war,
sent over to Japan to finish that one.
All the soldier boys who'd been away
and come back home had learned some of the things
that I had learned in Buffalo. On Cutshin
and up Laurel Holler everybody
miles around knew everybody everywhere
we walked, their first names, and their grandparents,
all their cousins, too. The world was bigger
than we knew, and it was moving in on us.

At home my brothers knew for sure I'd died
or maybe Dad had sold me. When I'd send them
store-bought things, a truck with wooden wheels (we
shipped our rubber to our boys across the seas),
they thought Mom charged the toys on time from
Dewey's store to fool them. Jimmy'd gone and come
back dead. My sister Becky was the only
one who said I'd never leave them, not for good.
Bea was a baby when I left, still was
when I came home, a crybaby at that.
Mom couldn't nurse her anymore with Helen
on the way, and gone were all the summer jars
I'd helped her fill. We lived on Dewey's
goodness—beans and fatback tasted fine to me.

My dad had only ever one job, at
the mines. It didn't last long, never seemed
to help the family anyway. He was
a hunter and a trapper; anything
his skins brought in had been already spent
down at the store. Even if we had to sell
the eggs our few hens laid, there'd be money
for tobacco. Thank God for corn and Sam,
our mule who'd haul it to the mill so Mom
could make bread we'd crumble in the beans, all
we'd have till dandelion weed greened up
come spring. But me, I would take home and Mom,
the boys and Becky, even whiny Bea,
over Buffalo any day you'd ask.

At last spring came. I loved to walk the mountains,
see how the little plants pushed their way through
earth and wonder how they could have the power
to come up through all that. Then it was to
work planting the crops of food. But we had
fresh wild greens that Mom taught us to find.
There's greens we cooked all day, then fried some more
to kill the poison from them, and greens we'd
wilt in lard and eat up nearly raw. We saved
beans for seed, and when we cut potatoes
for their eyes we were careful not to go
too deep to have some left to fry. But Mom
made sure we saved enough because she knew
without them that next winter we would starve.

What I brought back from Buffalo was mostly
thoughts I'd think inside my head. How could I
speak them? I learned there's people who don't sound
like us; they change our talk to be like theirs
just listening to them. That there were churches
that weren't Holiness or Baptist, and then what
Myrtle taught me most of all was that no
matter what good prayers some people pray,
it doesn't mean they truly are good people.
But, too I learned that mothers aren't supposed
to cry alone at night because of lack
of food enough to stop the hunger; sometimes
they fix their hair and go out with their husbands.
I wanted that for Mom, and for me, too.

If Dad was not the fool he was, we could've
had powdered milk, canned beef, dried beans and rice.
He only had to make his X, but he'd
not hold with give-aways from FDR
or Truman either. He'd not work the
WPA (the cursed Democrats),
but he would let his wife work near to death,
his children starve, pull up the onion sets
Mom's sister Martha gave; no handouts for him.
One morning Dad was screaming loud at Mom,
there's no wood for the cook stove, last night she
should have sent out one of us girls (never
the boys); it was her fault like always.
Just as he said he'd slap her 'cross the room,

I'd come in with an armload. I warned him
not to try it. He went for her, and I
went for his head, slinging a piece of wood.
He didn't hit my mom, but I did hit him.
Boy, was I in trouble, not for the first time,
not the last. But that's not why I went to
boarding school after the war was done for good;
that was Miss Shaw again, and Mom. At school
there was just me in seventh grade. I had
to choose between grade six which I'd done once
in Buffalo and eight—no grades after that.
My student days looked almost over; but Mom
would not let the story of her life be mine.
Again I'd leave to be the girl she wanted.

## Portrait of My Mother as a Piece of Coal

What was the weight of earth and
time that forged you? I only
see what time has worn away,
my own rough image
as if reflected on dark glass.
The living heart still beating
after what you were is gone.

# A Photograph Not Taken, Circa 1969

Even now I can't tell you
which was my granny's firstborn
and which Grandpa claimed as his
nor of the pair
which uncle was it used the kerosene
(or was it lighter fluid?)
to wipe the road tar from my town-girl feet
that could walk on broiling pavement
once even a smoldering cigarette
still wet from the inside of a stranger's lip
but not the gravel up the holler to their trailers
without tears
I didn't cry
at the burn of his oil-rimmed hands
or even later when my mother
pinched tight her lips
to hold back the scold
at me for my bare feet where they
had no business being or at whichever brother
(Cecil, Ted?)
for their country remedies
britches she'd long outgrown

Legacy

Barnacles on the mother
ship—those tiny frets and furies

piling one next to the other,
cozy-like, and always room for more.

Maybe it's her anger that will be last
to go—she will forget my name,

my father's ashes in his box still
by her bed, but not forget her ire.

Maybe, too, they have begun
to crust around my spine, and I

will carry on the mother
load when she is gone.

# What My Mother Can't Mend

Always my skin remembers
satin piping all the way around
the square yard or two of blanket
I would drag across the lawn
through gravel and mud,
tangling it around my chubby legs,
so you, Mother, usually the teller
of this tale, slipped it from
underneath me as I slept,
snipped it into manageable pieces,
not wanting to deprive me of what comfort
I could take outside your body,
but those dimpled knees
and how they gravitated down!

I made you sew it back together.
That's always how the story ends.
I knew you could fix anything, even
what you'd torn apart,
and must have trusted you
to make amends for any harm.
But here is what I wonder,
did I love it just as much
or did my fingers worry always
at the stitching? And now I watch you
try to patch together sentences,
drag memory from waking dream,
one thread of thought
found and lost again.

# The Long Way Home

# Journal Entry: February 2015

I spent most of yesterday at the ER torturing my mother. We shouldn't have gone. I knew we shouldn't have gone, and yet we went because we feared what we were seeing was a stroke or a seizure. Six hours of hell later we are given a name for the twitching and jerking—myoclonus—which means, as far as I can tell, twitching and jerking, and is caused by nobody knows: her new medication, as I suspect, or the dementia itself or just being old and tired. And all we accomplished is wearing out my mother enough that she finally slept, and maybe that is good enough.

She probably does not remember the trip to the ER, or lying in that uncomfortable bed for hours, her pain and blood pressure rising as the nurses refused to let us give the pills we brought with us, saying she might choke on them. She probably does not remember saying on the way to the hospital one of the few completely lucid statements I have heard from her over the last several days: "I think maybe we are jumping too high." Meaning "jumping the gun" by this trip to the ER.

I said, "Maybe we are, but we have to make sure you're okay." But of course, we didn't. She is not okay and she never will be again, and we didn't make sure of anything we didn't already know, and I am exhausted and angry at myself for putting her through this, and at the medical profession in general—at the ER docs and nurses and at the gerontology PA who at first seemed to be our savior and now is not returning my calls asking if it is possible the meds we are giving are hurting more than helping. And a sad kind of angry that the love between my mother and me is not a love that gives either of us comfort. Except sometimes.

Yesterday as my mother lay in bed twitching and moving her hands in response to some scene in her mind that she alone could see, I stood by her and ran my fingers through her thick, curly hair, soothing and petting and expressing a love she will not allow when awake. Not even now when we have crossed most other barriers: I dress her and help her position her floppy breasts into a too big bra. I even wiped her butt for her when she soiled herself not once but twice on the ER bed she was not allowed to get up from. No shame in this for her—only chaos and discomfort which hopefully will be forgotten. But forgotten too will be the tenderness of the touch accepted and given. When she woke up and saw me there she smiled and reached up to touch my hair, "That's a pretty gray hat you have on!" she told me.

I laughed and said, "Guess what, Mommy! That gray hat is my hair." I bent to let her feel it, and she ran her fingers through my curls as I had through hers, fluffing and "fixing" them for me, stroking me in a way that I seldom recall her doing as a younger mother to me, her curly-headed child.

One of my earliest memories is of waking to her cool hands on my chest and the smell of Vicks, and then asking the next morning if, should I cough in the night, would she come again? At bedtime that evening she brought me the blue jar, giving instructions on how to soothe myself.

It is my father's lap that I best remember; his arms around me if I cried. My mother was the "doer" of the family—the feeder, the fixer of broken dolls and burnt-out lamps, and if she loved us—and I believe that she did—that was the shape of that love.

Only later, after the birth of her grandchild perhaps, and after the dailiness of care was no longer her primary function, did she become a hugger: hellos, goodbyes, and not just to us, but to the friends we would bring to let her feed them. After I left home, all our phone calls ended with "I love you." I should be grateful—and I am—that the hugs and kisses, the declarations of love continue. She worries about me in these elaborate delusions made up of one part memory and nine parts the who-knows-what-it-is that goes on in her head.

But I miss my mommy. I miss the mother I had two weeks ago who instructed me on the fine art of coleslaw, the mother of six months ago who both required and resisted the necessary help in things like managing meds and paying bills, with her resentment and distrust of me, the new doer.

Even in her advancing dementia she is aware of what needs to be done—and that is the blessing and the curse: her habit of doing she remembers, but not the physical reality that she cannot anymore, and so ending up on the floor after trying to wipe up the pee she spilled from the bucket in the portable commode we placed near her bed as to prevent her from ending up on the floor.

Someday soon I will miss the mother who did that.

Aperture

In memory
my father is fixed now,
as in a photograph a year

or two before the fade.
Full-faced, crooked smile,
centered with me in the shot.

My mind won't settle
on a frame that holds my mother.
Flat images scatter to the floor.

## You Never Were

the mother I wanted at the time
I had you. Always I was
swallowing down the longing
rising for the mother
come and gone. The one

whose cool hand nested
in a tangle of my curls. The one
whose hair was blueblack
crow, caught midflight.
Once gravity had settled you

to ground, and I away
from you, I hungered
for the mother whose shovel
shouldered through red clay
to bring up bulbs I'd plant,

still clinging southern soil, in my
midwestern garden. Today it is
the mother who remembers
this I want, even as I hover
over you, my fingers

feathering the dark threads
woven through your gray.
I would cling
to whatever does not change
if I could find it.

# My Mother Tells Me What She Really Thinks

I am sorry I could not be that mother
you thought I should have been. I'm sorry I
was so tired after your brother came I could
hardly climb the stairs to read to you in bed.
I was not born knowing how to be a mother.
I learned mother knowledge from my mother,
caring for her younger ones. I was not
a child for long. My only time to be
alone was when I slept or walked to school.
The only time I had to read or write
was helping others learn. And in my marriage,
too, I let you children read when I should
have taught you to help me, so I could have
more time with you, but no, I did everything.

I did not want to do to you what had
been done to me. By aged seven, when a new
baby came, I cooked and did whatever
else was needed. I could never do enough
to please my dad. I'm sorry, Pauletta.
I think you had it pretty good. I hope
I showed and told you love. I never heard my
mother say it. I knew her work was love
keeping us alive. She let me learn to
help her. My love kept you from more you could
have learned. I wanted it all perfect
for you, and then I had to go and have
a baby brother and spoil it all. I hope
someday you'll know how hard motherhood is.

# The Girls in the Corners of My Mother's House
### (A poem for two voices)

don't come out when you're here,
wear the clothes
you long ago outgrew        are more real than

           what's left—
this broken body
I hardly know as mine,       the grownup children who
worry, worry,              worry about doctors and bills,
boxes of pills           so many pills,
morning, noon and night,    and what's lost next

my memory's cracked
to shards of glass
laid side by side, but

         can't be put back.

     So these girls in the corners

keep a sort of company       will only go away
when it's                 too
        late

## My Mother's PT

My mother at 80 has fallen
for a man my age whose job once was
to keep her on her feet.
He calls her Larnie-cane, a soft
tap to remind her that her own two legs
are not enough
to carry her anymore.
He phones her on his way
from one old lady
to the next. She says,
I think he's lonely,
trouble with his wife—I hope
she's not upset he's calling me.

# Where She Goes

*—A Cento*

Mother, you are folding into the deep
cave of the place inside you

where I am not.
My words like rocks

against the jagged walls
are dust before the bottom.

Can you be happy in that place
where, should you leave it,

everyone who died
must die again?

Mother, how am I to live
out here without you?

## Sleepwalking to Circa 1980

Best is that place my mother goes at night
to see us back where we belong—my brother
turns his plastic stereo up too loud
in the room, once mine, rear of the house (now
only the hearth remains); my niece, her wild
fine hair still blond, flings herself from the dresser
we gave years ago to Goodwill into
my sister's waiting arms. And me? I'm safe
away, leading a life she cannot see,
not presiding over hers. My father's heart
still beats for her, the beard she never liked
a stubbled gray. He blocks her passage from
one room he never lived in to the next,
tells her, *Sleep. We'll see you in the morning.*

## After My Father's Death,
##    My Mother Tells Him of Their Life Together

I remember the first time I saw you.
I had only been at Southland Bible
Institute three days. At supper, we new students
tried to size you old ones up. You in your
Combs High jacket, black and orange, teasing
everyone, and I thought several things about you,
but mostly I thought you were a smartass.
I was not looking to find a boyfriend.
I had one I didn't much want in
Korea, and anyone knew that a
girl didn't leave a soldier off at war.
And anyway we were there to become
good Christian girls, go out and spread the gospel,
not to find a husband, "Oh no, not that."

Really, I had no place to go. After
boarding school I'd gone back to Cutshin, helped Mom
from her surgery, got into it again
with Dad. He called Becky a whore just for
asking to go out with kids from church.
He waved his stick. I picked up a jar of
blackberries I'd canned, hit him on his shoulder,
hoping it would be his head. He was too
tall for that, but red went all down his left
side to his feet. He screamed that I had killed him.
He wasn't hurt. He wore those clothes for days,
showed what I'd done. I never spent another
night at home. Later I learned you didn't want
to be at Southland any more than I did.

You were a big shot, though, pastor of the church
and on the radio. You had a talent
for it. I remember going to that
Christmas party, thinking, what a waste of time.
I was ready to go home, get away
from the pressure of being holy, which
I couldn't pull off very well. There I
sat alone, and so were you. You asked to
sit by me, and I thought, What does he want?
I'd been warned, watch out, the love-and-leave type.
You asked about my life, and I thought,
he is smooth. I'll ask him, too. You let it all
pour out; my heart broke open. Up the cow path
to the women's dorm, I kept you in my mind.

Oh, that hour with you went so fast. We talked
about so many things—your call from God—
and I was never sure I was called to
anything; I told you that. I was there
because I needed to be some place other
than where I was, and for you, everyone
who mattered died—your mother a faded
photograph, your grandmother's last words to you,
"Be good." Your drunk father slinking past your
door at night and how we both agreed
Southland was just a starting place for us.
How you loved books and learning everything
you found in them. It was not wrong to search
for something more. After that night, talk buzzed,

Hansel and Lewis. I loved it. Next day
when morning classes ended, you asked me
to walk with you the long way. I was so
happy when that letter from Korea
came breaking it off so I didn't have to.
I asked you to the mission back on Cutshin
and Christmas Eve who should hitchhike his way in,
but you. I was surprised, but Miss Shaw and
the other ladies didn't seem to be.
We played Candyland. And later Ted, my
brother, showed up drunk down at the clinic
where they had you sleep. The big shock, though, came
New Year's Eve, when the preacher asked for my
betrothed to come up and say a few words.

We had yet to hold hands. Later you told me
you had nearly jumped through your skin, but
mostly hoped I'd go along with it. I thought,
he hasn't asked me yet. You never did.
But when you started talking of a name
for our first child, I knew you meant business.
Renée, rebirth, boy or girl. By New Year's
next we were married. Our first kiss was not
till summer when I taught Vacation Bible
School on Cutshin and you couldn't stay away,
so in the little church that I helped build
you kissed me. Our first married kiss was in
Cawood, where your people lived. None of them came.
It didn't matter; we were our family now.

## How They Leave Us

Nearly a decade
since my mother and I
sat together on the couch
beside the chair that held
my father's body, waiting
for the undertaker.

I didn't cry
until we finally covered him
with the quilt from their bed
and decided to pick up a bit for company.
I think it was his walker
that folded me
to the floor. My mother
knelt beside me, relieved
a little of her own
as she held mine.

> Maybe it was then I thought
> that I could bear his death
> but never hers.

We never know
what we can hold
until it's on us
and we splinter,
or don't.

I didn't know there would be
other ways to lose a mother.

Some days she wanders
through her rooms for hours
pulling clothes from closets,
folding them into suitcases.

I don't know where it is she goes
then or how much of her
will return.

I pat the cushion on the couch
beside me—*Why don't you wait
here with me
until it's time to leave?*

Portrait of My Mother
    as a Discarded Bird's Nest

in my hand unraveling.
Pieces crumble
to my page. I can see
the seam, the two sides knit together,
but I can't make it hold.
A softness at the center remains.

Winter Trees

When my mother says
she likes the look of winter
trees (bonebare and black
against the gray scrubbed sky)

I take it for the gift it is
to tell me that she loves
a thing she still can have.
We take the long way

home through empty streets,
oak and maple,
mulberries' twisted
limbs angling toward the earth.

It's not enough. It's what I have
to give her.

# Journal Entry: March 2015

On Monday I yelled at my 82-year-old mother with dementia because she wouldn't sit down on the toilet. She said she needed to use the bathroom but she wouldn't pull her pants down and sit. Before that, I had spent the morning patiently placing her hands on the handles of her walker, leading her through doors and down hallways, positioning her in one direction or another for the successful completion of various tasks I am only now becoming aware of as tasks: sitting on a chair, finding the fork, placing not just one but both feet on the floor in order to rise.

"Here!" I snapped. "Sit here!" and slapped the toilet seat hard.

"Okay!" she said, beginning to move away from the toilet toward the closed bathroom door.

"Where are you going, Mom?"

"Somebody knocked on the door."

"No," I said, regrouping. "That was me. I hit the toilet seat too hard. Do you need to use the bathroom?"

"Why, yes!"

"Then let's sit down right here."

Let off the hook for my loss of control, I regained it by the age-old ploy of mothers, nurses and middle-aged daughters: though it's your butt in the seat, your runny mashed potatoes on the plate, your $6000-a-month room in the assisted living facility, always "you" are "we."

Except when I'm not there.

I wanted for my mother to live with us. When it became clear that her living situation with our cousin as her companion was falling apart, I wanted for us—my husband, mother and me—to live together with the help of paid assistants. We looked for houses to replace her too-small ranch and our no-first-floor-bed-or-bath Tudor. We didn't find anything soon enough to meet our location, price, condition qualifications. And so my mother is in an efficiency apartment—a glorified room—in the assisted living memory care unit of a care facility—a glorified nursing home—and I am trying to come to grips with what I have done to her in my attempt to do well for her.

Each visit I learn more about my limitations: some physical, as in the challenges of moving her to where she is unable to get on her own, and some emotional. I am learning something about patience—not only that mine does not fill the deepest well, but that it does not come alone: patience and grief, patience and anger, patience and humor at the oddball positions we get into. And I am learning, too, that I like to go home to my clean, quiet house or on an impromptu date with my husband.

I like to think that if we had moved in together it would have been a disaster.

I don't like to think that I alone could have saved her from this fate.

The two thoughts don't cancel each other out, but live in an uneasy truce inside me. All I can do is not enough. My mother is dying. And that's not the worst of it. She is dying bit by bit, confused, not particularly happy and, despite expensive care and daily visits from those who love her, she is dying alone. This is the best I could do.

# Who Do I Think I Am?

## After Your Diagnosis of Dementia

You tell again the story
of the blanket I dragged everywhere
through grass and mud, the one
my hands remember,
satin piping
just begun to fray.
But you say
*she,*
as if I'm not
that girl, the stubborn one
who made you stitch back together
the blanket cut so I'd not trail it
quite so far behind.
*She,*
as if we are no longer
mother, daughter.
*She,*
as if I'm the one
shedding the self I've been.

## The Hospital

I cannot find my mother.
I am not dreaming, but might as well be—
darkened halls, a constant beep and clang, that
wailing woman,
not mine but surely someone's,
who lies invisible
beneath the thin sheet's rise and fall.

Beneath the thin sheet's rise and fall
who lies invisible?
Not mine, but surely someone's
wailing woman,
darkened halls, a constant beep and clang that
I am not dreaming, but might as well be.
I cannot find my mother.

## Portrait of My Mother as the Moon

Imagine the Moon broke apart in orbit.
Would the chunks of the Moon
still pull the Earth?
Obviously the tides would change.
Would this cause the Earth
to wobble subtly back and forth,
like the Moon is doing now.
Or would the Earth
just keep going like always,
the mass of the Moon,
the gravity of it
still there?
Imagine the same scenario,
but this time the Moon's mass
escapes Earth's orbit
and floats into space,
so mass and gravity are lost.
What would happen to the Earth then?

## The View from There

Where in the world
does my mother go, eyes
shut so tight her lower lashes
curl in toward a view
that's hers alone?
Yesterday she told
me—*after the rains, the winds
came,* and this morning
that's what they do.

# Who Do I Think I Am?

A.
A red peony transplanted
midbloom (say, from the yard around
your mother's emptied house into your own)
wilts and will not blossom
for two seasons.
Maybe more.

B.
I wheel my mother
around the nursing home. She has left
the doll they've given her
(the prettiest girl she's ever seen)
resting on her bed.
"Where's your baby, Larnie?"
asks the nurse. I answer,
"Here I am."

C.
On the day I do not visit
my mother asks, "Do you think
my mother is coming today?"

My Mother Briefly Reunites
    with Her Dead Sister Becky
    in the Body of Me and Tells Us

Life is small,
but it isn't.
You are so pretty, your hair
worn now like mine.
I love you.

# Family Photograph

I don't like to look at you
slumped in that damn
wheelchair in the nursing home,
your lips a single slice,
persimmon red,
to match the sweater
that once fit you
just fine.

We've taken turns
for pictures with you;
my aunt and I,
our hips, plump
fruit, stretch out
to fill the frame around
your peach pit
of a face.

# Red

On Christmas Eve, we pulled matching ribbons
from boxes holding matching coats she'd sewed
for us, and one for her, red wool that didn't scratch,
black velvet trim. She could make anything. She loved

red in any season, and later purple jackets she'd adorn
with ruby rhinestones on the lapels. Even now, boxed inside
her mind, a splash of color's all it takes, sometimes, to pull
her toward the world—*Oh my,* she'll say, *how beautiful!*

## My Mother's Clothes

Still far too many blouses and slacks
even though we reduced them by half
the first move to the home, and half again
the next, saving only those that almost fit,

like her skin, lying loose against her bones.
There is so little left. Even her wedding ring
I've tucked inside my father's in my dresser drawer,
her gardening hat on a shelf in my closet.

## Portrait of My Mother as a Dried Sunflower

The round shape of you
no longer round,
bent in on yourself
as if you are trying to find your way
back to the place you began.
You smell of dust
and still that scent
of only you.
I cannot see what you were
in what I have before me,
though in dreams you still stand
tallest in the field.
Every day a little
more of you
is gone. You are
beautiful.
You are so beautiful.
At the center,
a constellation of seeds
never planted.

## Too Personal

like the underside
of a cat's tongue, like
someone else's bathwater,
like bedsheets still warm, like
a spit-wet thumb flicking sleep
from the corner of your mother's
eye, like an old hymn hummed
beneath curdled breath, like
ragged stitches pulled from
a wound. These poems are
too personal.

## Last Night the Moon

that ragged moon
       through my window
                    the moon
         drew out what was left
of my waiting breath
     (my heart breath, longing…)
sucked it out of me
         into the purple length of sky
              with greenwood stuttering sparks
              it grew
                   a fiery howl.
You heard it.
                    Across the midnight hiss of highways
I know you heard
              that breath wanting
          only
      the intimate coil
of your ear.

# What Comes

Quiet together
when a soft cracked hymn
comes climbing the cords
of your frayed voice,
spills from the mouth
wiped clean
of the meal I fed you

and I am afraid

I will never remember
how it felt to be a daughter,
yours—
every picture
in the album
reversed, a mirror
  holding me
  holding you.

# Pentimento (Journal Entries: Summer 2015)

There are five sets of doors between me and my mother. The first two doors are sliding doors, and automatic, though they are not always triggered to open if it is a wheelchair rather than a standing person moving through first. The third door pulls outward. It is human powered, and unlocked. The fourth, I unlock with a key card and walk past the elevator doors to my left that lead to the Assisted Living section of Memory Care where my mother began her stay before flunking out a couple of weeks later. Never mind, we didn't like it up there anyway. The staff was unfriendly, and the private duty aides sat clicking their freshly polished nails on their cell phones as the elders gathered around the nurses' station, not talking to each other or even to themselves.

The last door pushes inward after a swipe of my card, and it is here I stop and smile, no matter how I am feeling. I try never to enter with the sadness I carry with me on my face or to show dismay at whatever I see inside those doors. It is getting easier to smile now that there's less likelihood of finding my mother parked in a wheelchair. Now often she is up and staggering about with an aide, or sitting on one of the many couches or at a table, talking near, if not with, others. And sometimes she is smiling even before she sees me.

Going out those doors is more difficult. If I am leaving with my mother in her wheelchair ("I am your motor," I tell her), it is the complicated dance of butt first and a quick turn as not to use my mother's feet as the doorstop (sometimes the turn becomes a swerve, and I tell her that her driver is drunk). Then those feet go first through the next door, this time my shoulder holding it open. From there, it depends on where we are heading; usually we turn right, to the courtyard door, which opens with a push of a button, as long as there's no elder in her own wheelchair blocking the way.

If I am leaving alone, I kiss my mother goodbye and hope it is not her brave face I am seeing, lips tight as not to have them tremble before she cries. If I am lucky it is her don't-bother-me-with-kisses-I'm-fine face.

My husband says it's like sending your children to kindergarten, hoping they'll be happy, learn a lot, not get in fights. But kids in kindergarten get to come home.

\*\*\*

I am studying my mother for signs of the woman she was underneath the layers of dementia. They are there. Today at lunch she snapped at me for pushing food on her. "Pauletta!" she said sharply, and my hand with the fork went back down to the table. Quickly! No questions asked. A rare opportunity to be a scolded daughter.

\*\*\*

"Larnie was busy, busy, busy today!" the nursing home aide tells me. My mother wants so much to be the busy woman she was. She is always touching things, moving things. Considered a fall risk, the staff tried to keep Mom in her wheelchair for most of her first couple of months here. I believe it was her persistence, rather than my advocacy, that has loosened their resolve. She has not given up. It would be easier for everyone around her if she did. But she hasn't yet, and though after my visits I am exhausted from chasing her as she lurches around the nursing home, I am grateful that her feistiness remains.

***

I am not sure what I thought it was that would be last to go. Love, I suppose. That she would know us and want to be with us, her family—and that is all still true. She usually knows me, though the context of where we are and what we are doing here is often lost. Maybe there are some things that her mind chooses not to know.

***

They have given my mother a baby doll to calm her down. Even a few months ago, when she first arrived, I wouldn't have believed that my mother would have had anything to do with such an obvious ploy. Sure, she sees children we don't see, but she wouldn't see a living, breathing child when we see a plastic toy, would she? Apparently she would. It's the prettiest baby she's ever seen, she'll say as she coos happily and cuddles him—then holds him by one leg and drops him to the floor. If it works to curb Mom's ratcheting anxiety, it's fine with me. Better baby dolls than tranquilizers. Though some days she has both.

One day I walked into my mother's room and saw a mother I have never seen before. The crying mother was bad enough. This was the scrapping mother, hitting her hands at the aide and telling her she'd never amount to anything, just like her mother. The aide looked at me and said, "Well, she's right about my mother." The further Mom sinks into dementia the more startling are her moments of psychic clarity.

I said, "Mom, don't talk that way to her. She's my buddy. She'd never do anything to hurt you."

"She grabbed me by the throat and tried to strangle me!"

"Mom, she did not."

I sat beside her on her bed and put my arm around her for a while. "Let's get out of here," I said, getting up to gather the things we needed. "Here's your hat." I put it on her head. "What's your hurry?" A joke funny only to me.

We did our daily ritual of leaving the locked unit to sit in the shade in the facility's courtyard, her in a wheelchair and me in a wrought iron garden chair. We talked about the daylilies that have sprung up through the creeping phlox that was blooming in the early days of our visits, about the ever-present wall lizards and the robin hopping from one place to the next. "Well, who knew robins really do go bob-bob-bobbing along," I said and she laughed when I sang the song.

"All right now?" I asked.

"Yes," she said. "But don't tell me something didn't happen when I say so."

"Okay," I said. "It's a deal. Let's shake on it." And we did.

*** 

My mother and I talk more than we used to. We have both always had the knack for silence. When I was young and at home, she was too busy for much conversation, and my nose was usually in a book. I loved the rare occasions when she would sit with her sisters around a table and tell stories about me as if I was not there to hear.

Much later, after my father died and we lived again in the same town, though not the same house, our weekly dinners centered around her favorite shows—*Jeopardy* and *Antiques Roadshow*. We would go antiquing and wander the aisles as often apart as together. We chatted in the car and in her living room, or mine, but we could sit quietly for hours. And as mother's dementia progressed she talked less and less in company; she became the listener at the table as her family told stories about her.

And then there was the phase when I felt I must argue with everything she said, as if by will alone I could force away her delusions. Now that I'm learning to agree with everything, instead, there is an ease to our conversation:

"Is that right?"

"Well, that must have been something!"

"No, I haven't seen Daddy today."

Mostly, my responses are based on tone, rather than content. She speaks very low, and fast and even when I do hear her, I can't always decipher what she says. When she speaks clearly, it can be as if I'm eavesdropping on her half of a conversation and I am struggling to keep up.

"What did you put in his pail for dinner?" she asked me the other day.

"Half-runner beans and new potatoes," I said. "But I was too lazy to make the cornbread."

One morning she said, apropos of nothing I knew, "She went to sleep and didn't wake up."

"Who," I asked.

"Your old teacher."

There is no way she could have known that Mrs. De-Hoag had died a week or two before.

"I don't know how you know these things," I told her.

"I don't either," Mom said. "Sometimes it just starts as something small, like I see John on a skateboard."

"That sounds like a good memory to me," I say, and leave it there. "Should we go have some lunch?"

\*\*\*

Today, pulling her pants back up after a trip to the toilet, I notice the folds and folds of skin from her far-too-rapid weight loss. They will never again be filled, and yet will never rest comfortably against her bones without the flesh that once filled them.

*** 

And too, I am learning a new sort of language, that of touch. I never thought to realize how touch-deprived my mother must have been in the eight years since my father's death. She began receiving weekly massages a few years ago, but it was not until the move to the nursing home intensified her already increasing anxiety that touch became part of her daily life. She is never so calm as when someone's hands are on her. We all brush her hair, stroke her back, hold her hand. Sometimes I climb onto her narrow bed behind her and she'll pull my hand up to her chest and hold it as she must have held my father's hand, as I hold my husband's as we spoon into sleep. It doesn't last long. She's not much of a napper. But, for a moment or two, she is at peace, and so am I.

# The Real Story

## The Real Story

No one tells you how old you'll be someday, old
enough to be mother to your mother. Your father, mean-
while, left the party early, before the need for pulling
down the rafters, boxing the whole thing up—ash now
in his own last box, died with his last book sliding out of
his lap, and it's come down to you to figure out the real
story—did the flu shot really give her the flu that year, you
away living your child-free, parent-free life, and somebody
wants to know, now she's in a nursing home, pulling off
her shoes, putting them on again. She still knows enough
to know there is no sense—nonsense—in this, she still
can laugh as you bend to slip the left one back on over the
sock, pink from the wash, you have labeled with her name.
Nobody said you would watch as the flesh from which
your flesh was made dissolves away.

Her loss, your gain: all she will not eat congregates
beneath your skin and you grown wide enough for both
of you, large enough to hold her, your body curves its own
*Pieta* for a mother there and not. No one said your hand
will push what food she'll take between her pressed lips,
your hand will be the one rubbing her head as she sits on
the toilet forgetting why she is there, *push it out, Mommy,
let it go*. No one says how long it takes, or what is lost
along the way, how you forget how to be daughter and
only know *right now, right now*, the way she does. No one
says the pain is not forgetting, but remembering.

## What My Mother Can't Forget

Today the bird trapped inside
her forgets how to sing, but
flutters, sharp angles, from throat
to rib to spine to pelvic
bone. She grabs my hand, "It is
time to go home," she tells me,
pauses, "the one I don't have."

## Self-Portrait as Ellipsis

I live at the cliff edge
of story, the pause
between language
and the hand's blind reach.
In the photograph
I am the vee of light
between the shadows
two bodies make.
I am the words
you might have said.

## The Problem Is

with our hands, the way they can never
be still—my mother always tugging
some invisible fold in the fabric,
drawing it in, and I am smoothing down
the pants leg she has pulled past the impossible
swell of her ankle up to her tinkertoy knee,
then fluffing the curls
of her hair, licking my thumb
to rub lunch away. The problem is

she is rearranging a world
imperceptible to me while I muddle around
in the one she's forgotten. *Hand me that,*
she'll say, and I'll pluck at the air, useless
as I was when she would send me

back from the car for the sweater
she'd end up having to go for anyway,
saying, *Why am I the only one*
*in this house who ever sees*
*what's in plain sight?* The problem is

the door between
has opened just enough
for two hands to pass through,
neither of them mine.

# The Body / Above It

## I.

We cannot see what she sees. At night dark
insects slip inside the shoes our mother
will shake out come morning. Her bedside clock
runs backwards. We cannot smell the burning
lingering around the box of ash and bone
that was our father. To us bread only
tastes of bread. We lay fleshy cheeks against
the rumpled angles of her face, whisper
goodnight, then come to visit her again,
taut skin and buds of breasts barely rippling our
tie-dyed shirts. We are more real to her
in dreams than hovering near her in our
clumsy bodies, refused entrance to her world,
slowly crumbling behind her mind's locked door.

## II.

Just inside her new nursing home's locked door
my mother lists awkward in her wheelchair,
adrift—one sock and both cloth shoes scattered
helplessly behind. I bend to gather
them up and say into the ear that holds
her last remaining hearing aid, "You are my
diddle, diddle dumpling," forever hoping
she will remember the rest of the rhyme.
It, too, is gone—no later, alligator,
no after while—sunk to a bottomless
bottom, nestled beside, some days, my name.
Now, my mother rubs her heel and whispers
maybe to me, "It is dying." "Your foot?"
I ask her. "No, the body above it."

## III.

The body, too, continues its descent.
Each week a little more disintegrates
from sagging folds of skin that held plump weight
of mother love cooked up in iron skillets—
a taste of bread, a bite of beans before
she'd hand the plates around. I am the one
these days who never can be full—my hunger
is enough for both of us—pound by pound
I take into my body all she's lost.
The pain for years she carried low, a belt
wrapped just beneath her spine, she never speaks
a word of now. It's mine. I wear the ache
my mother has discarded. Still she cries,
and when I ask, she can't remember why.

IV.

She can't remember why she's there, or where
there is—some days it is the hospital
where she'd not let my father die. The chair
beside his bed became her own—she would
not have him wake alone to dark and those
red blinking lights. Small mercy, I suppose,
that she's forgotten, now, his death at home.
We cleared their desk and found the words she wrote:
*I see him in his chair cocooned in white—*
*the bedspread I crocheted. It seemed to me*
*he winked and smiled his little crooked smile.*
*I caught a wisp of his own scent as he*
*floated by and thought, no matter his poor*
*feet don't work, he won't need them anymore.*

## V.

Her feet don't work more days than not, these days
they wrap themselves one foot around the other,
her legs tied up in knots. It would take days,
back then, for Mother to untie those other
knots crocheted with thread and yarn, her lips pursed
tight—mistakes were fine for others, just not
for her. The small hook flew, the threads dispersed
to right the wrongs she saw and we did not.
Now there's a world of wrong she sees, we don't.
Her life's become a living hell on wheels—
from wall to wall she rolls her chair, eyes shut
against the crush of all her failures,
her mouth a clenched knot of concentration,
off in wild search of threadbare consolation.

## VI.

I once believed there would be consolation
in her things. We kept for her the poppies
painted in that shade of orange mixed only
in the years we all remember—five around
the maple table—hung it up above
the shelves filled with the teapots that we chose
for her as best. Eyes open or eyes closed
she doesn't see them. She taught me to take
comfort in what's left—my father's books,
Granny's mixing bowls. But no solace lives
in memory now. Take from my own shelves
all passed from my mother's hands into mine.
Pull down the curtains she crocheted. The only
ease is skin on skin. I breathe her into me.

## VII.

Your purse breathed out Jergens lotion, crumpled
tissues, loose change and Wrigley's Spearmint gum.
Never carried more than what was needed.
Never needed anything that was not
slung across your shoulder as we walked, my
hand raised to yours before I'm running up
ahead, always knowing you'll be back there
with your purse—clutched years later on your lap,
the same three dollars from last week's car trip
never came untucked. When did you stop buying
the gum you'd pass to me? When did you start
to trail those tissues I still find beneath
the floor mat of my car? When's the last time
you said, "Get me my purse, and take me home."

VIII.

Should we take this one or let it go? In one hand I weigh
a cup, tea stains spidering around a needle-thin crack.
Her favorite cup. She's forgotten now this kitchen's
blue-trimmed cupboards, this house edged with
roses where underneath a fault line rumbled
faint for years, unheard. Tremors beneath
the fragile bone, beloved ground. Shards
of who she was are almost visible
between her skin and mine. The
clink of cup upon the counter,
light as a twig snap, light as
her sleeping breath still
punctuating
air.

# In the Dementia Unit

stealing sugar
    from your sweet cheeks
my little mommy     baby girl
    I'll never have    not from my
  body you are traveling
back into           all     I can do is
    love          what is left
time        slows no     our bodies
   slow           time
   ticks on   I look  away from you
an hour     has passed      a day
when I am with you I forget   (how do
   I count)   the ways
you are already gone

## My Mother Makes Her Amends

At LaRosa's, of all places, with the plastic
forks and paper napkins pulled away
from her restless reach. After I feed her
the salad, but before the bacon pizza,
she lets it go.
How could I have known
that she too, grieved
for me, her baby girl,
these fifty-three years
since she brought my brother home?
I'd heard the story: released
from the hospital into a rare
November snow, no chains
on Daddy's tires, the neighbor's
rescue in a four-wheel drive
across Pine Mountain, how
my mother's slippered feet left craters
through the yard, my brother wrapped
up in her cloth car coat. How,
selfish girl, I'd turned my back.

I was four.
I remember only being fed the story
of how I never wanted him to stay,
how I never wanted
much from anybody, anyway.
I'd learned to rock myself to sleep
in my own red rocking chair.

She tells me now, pushing out each word
to make the first full sentences
I've heard from her in months,
eyes locked on mine to be sure
I hear her this time:
*There was a storm. I had to decide*
*which one, and he was the one*
*I didn't even know yet.*
*I tried to be fair.*
I say, in my daughter-
to-mother-with-dementia voice,
*That sounds fair to me.*

The light from her eyes
blinds me. I feel the rush
of time spooled backwards,
the elemental pull
of infant in her arms. The necessity
of tenderness makes mothers of us all.
*Do you think so?*
She reaches both hands
to the child I was,
brings my face to hers for a kiss.
Whatever else to say
dissolves beneath the table
between us.

## What Doesn't Change

My mother's wicked twinkle
when she laughs. How she goes,
*Umm, uh, uh, umm, uh,*
when she worries
and will not say why.
If I could live inside
her brain, I'd know
how everything has changed—

collapsed tunnels light will never
see again, skittering mice
that gnaw the fragile walls
away. That I name this in metaphor
does not change
except when it does.
When what is, is. I make

the best of it. Paint her nails
with bright colors she loved,
comb her hair just enough
to leave the curls and laugh
when she laughs because it doesn't
really matter what's so funny now.
My love for her has changed. It used to

flow uneasily, a moat with bridges
to be lowered and raised.
Now it is a river
wide enough for barges.
Touching hands across, we float
downstream, heading for the same
destination, though she'll be first
to reach dry land.

## Strawberry Moon

This morning's first waking
as light eases through
whatever opening it finds
and the owl's low question pulls
me from sleep. I don't remember
my dreams anymore, not as I did,
enthralled by my own
night wisdom spiraling
from sleep's deep spring.
Now I wake
with worry, knowing what I know
is never enough. My mother
still knows me most of the time
and mostly that is enough—that she
knows me as I knew her
before words, as *touch* and *safe*
and the giver of food that I ease
between the lips that open and close,
open and close. The strawberry moon
slips behind a cloud,
spilling its light as it goes.

# A Photograph Not, to My Knowledge
## Taken, 1953

The sapling boy who'll be my father
sits knees bent, leaning toward her
on the evening grass.
Pant cuffs flap his knobby ankles;
his hands exclaim
in the spring-damp air between them.
She cocks her head, her ear
his cup of words. My mother's eyes
hold distant hills; how they shimmer, new green.
Her skirt spreads in pleats and folds
around her. She takes his hand—
with the right breeze they'll rise
and spin away from us
into the waiting night.

## After the Dance

from chair to chair—the lurching
rise to my arms, the shuffled
turn, rock back, *bend your knees, it's*
*right behind you now*—my mother
draws my hand down to her cheek,
cradles some helpless thing she
thinks she holds—*hush now, I'm here.*

# NOTES

"My Mother Remembers Buffalo, 1944-45," "My Mother Tells Me What She Really Thinks" and "After My Father's Death, My Mother Tells Him of Their Life Together" are written using text from the memoir my mother wrote in 2006-2007 as nearly daily letters to my recently dead father. "My Mother Remembers Buffalo, 1944-45" is crafted as though spoken by a younger voice but includes many direct quotes from her text. "My Mother Tells Me What She Really Thinks" and "After My Father's Death, My Mother Tells Him of Their Life Together" are almost entirely her phrasing, though edited for length and cohesion, among other things. "The Body / Above It, IV" also includes a direct quote from her writing.

The final lines of "You Never Were" are from an unpublished poem by the late Leslie Cannon, written in response to Naomi Shihab Nye's "Trying to Name What Doesn't Change." "What Doesn't Change" is also in response to Nye's poem.

"Where She Goes" is composed of lines from the following poets, as well as my own: Rita Coleman, Diane Germaine, Linda Busken Jergens, Claudia Skutar. Diane Germaine's lines are also in her poem, "What Is it About Fall?".

"Portrait of My Mother as the Moon" is an erasure from a post by the user "Megatarius" on the online CosmoQuest Forum.

"The Real Story" includes phrases found in Ada Limón's *Bright Dead Things*.

# ACKNOWLEDGMENTS

Thanks to the publications in which versions of the following poems first appeared:

*Stirring: A Literary Collection*: "My Mother Has Stopped Telling Me She Loves Me"

*Still: The Journal*: "Portrait of My Mother's Dementia as Saturn's Rings" and "Palindrome"

*Appalachian Journal*: "My Mother Remembers Buffalo, 1944-45"

*The Messenger is Sudden Thunder: Selections from Lexington Poetry Month 2016*: "My Mother Briefly Reunites with Her Dead Sister, Becky, in the Body of Me and Tells Us"

*This Wretched Vessel* (Anthology of the 2014 Lexington Poetry Month Project, Accents Publishing): "Portrait of My Mother as a Dried Sunflower"

*& Grace: selections from Lexington Poetry Month 2015* (Accents Press, Spring 2016): A section of "The Body / Above It, IV"

*Pine Mountain Sand & Gravel, Volume 20* (Southern Appalachian Writers Cooperative and Dos Madres Press, 2017): "The Body / Above It, VIII"

Earlier drafts of the following poems first appeared on Accents Publishing's Lexington (Kentucky) Poetry Month Blog:

"My Mother's PT" (2013); "Portrait of My Mother as a Dried Sunflower" (2014); "Aperture," "The Body / Above It, V and VII," "Who Do I Think I Am?" (2015); "Too Personal," "Union Terminal: The Whispering Fountain," "Portrait of My Mother as a Piece of Coal," "My Mother Briefly Reunites With Her Dead Sister, Becky, in the Body of Me and Tells Us" (2016); "The View From There," "My Mother's Clothes," "Strawberry Moon" (2017)

An expanded version of "Pentimento" will appear in the anthology, *Memoirs of the Feminine Divine: Voices of Power & Invisibility*

I am grateful to Linda Parsons and Thomas Alan Holmes for their editing advice (all remaining punctuation and grammar errors are my own) and to Pamela Gibbs Hirschler, Douglas Van Gundy and Melissa Helton for their help with last minute decisions on individual poems. Dale Marie Prenatt, Laura Krystal, Savannah Sipple, Kelly Thomas and John Ray Sheline's assistance with the transcription of my mother's letters made it possible for her voice to be present in this book.

Many thanks, too, to Richard Hague, an early and often advocate of this book, and of all my work; to Jeanne Bryner, Robert Gipe, and George Ella Lyon for their careful reading and kind words; to my poetry students—who are also my teachers—for writing alongside me throughout these poems; to the Southern Appalachian Writers Cooperative for its nearly lifelong support; and to Robert and Elizabeth Hughes Murphy of Dos Madres Press, who give body to the breath of these words.

And gratitude beyond words to our cousin Gail Hughes, my mother's most faithful and dear companion; to Mom's beloved caregivers, Shenise, Evarest, Regina and Elisha; to my sibs Renée and John; to the "Lewis women"; and to my husband, Owen: you lived these poems.

## PHOTO CREDITS

iv Owen Cramer, 2017
86 Joseph Enzweiler, 1997
90 Charles Hansel, 1962
91 Probably Edith Shaw, circa 1942 (top)
   Probably Edith Shaw circa 1938 (bottom)
92 Probably Edith Shaw, circa 1940 (top)
   Unknown, circa 1955 (middle)
   Unknown, circa 1975 (bottom)

Need I say it?
## *This book is for Mom*
(the original palindrome)

# BIOGRAPHICAL NOTES

PAULETTA HANSEL was born in Richmond, Kentucky, the middle child of Larnie Lewis and Charles Hansel. Her poems and prose have been featured in journals including *Atlanta Review, Talisman, Appalachian Journal, Appalachian Heritage* and *Still: The Journal,* and on *The Writer's Almanac* and *American Life in Poetry.* She is author of five previous poetry collections, most recently *Tangle* (Dos Madres Press, 2015), and is managing editor of *Pine Mountain Sand & Gravel,* the literary publication of the Southern Appalachian Writers Cooperative. Pauletta has been involved with the Southern Appalachian Writers Cooperative since its earliest years, and was a member of the Soupbean Poets Collective out of Antioch/Appalachia in the 1970s. She is a Core Member of the Urban Appalachian Community Coalition and has served as Writer in Residence at Thomas More College and at WordPlay Cincinnati. She leads writing workshops and retreats in the Greater Cincinnati area and beyond. In April 2016, she was named the City of Cincinnati's first Poet Laureate. Pauletta lives with her husband, Owen Cramer, in Cincinnati. More information at https://paulettahansel.wordpress.com/.

*Author photo by Richard Hague.*

Other books by Pauletta Hansel
published by Dos Madres Press

First Person (2007)
What I Did There (2011)
Tangle (2015)


She is also included in:
Realms of the Mothers:
The First Decade of Dos Madres Press - 2016

For the full Dos Madres Press catalog:
www.dosmadres.com